ARCO-AIRCAM AVIATION SERIES

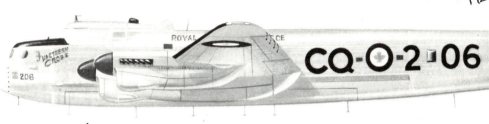

1
10–N, FM206, CQ–206. "Northern Cross". Central Navigation School, Summerside, Prince Edward Island, 1953.

AVRO LANCASTER
IN UNIT SERVICE

**By Mike Garbett
and Brian Goulding**

**Illustrated by
Mike Roffe**

ACKNOWLEDGEMENTS

This book is devoted to the men who built, flew and maintained the Lancaster (or "Lanc." as it became known) during its twenty-two years of service. Many have over the years delved deeply into their memories, diaries and albums. As a result, we have been able to disclose, perhaps, a few new sidelines on the Lancaster; also to illustrate the book with photographs, most of which, we hope, will be entirely new to readers—not an easy claim these days. Not all the photographs are of the best quality, particularly those illustrating the rarer units and variations in markings. We have not endeavoured to illustrate every unit, as markings were highly standardized. Space precludes coverage of special, experimental, test bed and civil variants.

Those who have entrusted their material to us, such as photographs and nose emblems actually removed from aircraft are named in the captions. To all who have contributed we extend our thanks. In particular we must mention:—Harry Holmes and other staff at Avro's, including Messrs. Ashwell, Dale, Houghton, Jack, Lawson, Page, Russell and Waterfall. Also—Trevor Allen, Chris Ashworth, Jack Gregson, Olive Hamilton, Bob Jones, Derek Monk, Cyril Parrish, Jim Patrick, John Rawlings, Bruce Robertson, Ray Sturtivant, W. J. G. Verco, M.V.O. (of the College of Arms), W/Cdr. Alan Walker and Chas Waterfall.

2
BII LL670, J9–P. 1668 Heavy Conversion Unit. Bottesford, January 1945. Note the still faintly visible G–H bars on the fin & 'Ops' score on the nose.

PUBLISHED BY

Arco Publishing Company, Inc., 219 Park Avenue South, New York, N.Y. 10003

First Published by Osprey Publications Ltd., and Printed in Great Britain

Library of Congress No. 78 93934 · Library Edition SBN 668 02118-7 · Paperback Edition SBN 668 02117-9

Copyright © Osprey Publications Ltd. 1970

BII DS713, OW–J, 426 ("Thunderbird") Squadron, RCAF, Linton-on Ouse, 16/8/43, the day before the Squadron first operated with the type (a night attack on the Rocket Establishment at Peenemünde). Note bulged bomb bay—A feature of most BIIs.   (E. C. G. Jones)

A veteran takes to the air. Bl R5868, PO–S of 467 Squadron, RAAF, taking off on it's 100th operation, Bourg-Leopold in Belgium, on the night of 10/11 May 1944. Skipper on this occasion was Plt/Off. T. N. Scholefield, RAAF. This Lanc exists to this day and stands at the entrance to Scampton from where it first flew with 83 Squadron. H2S radar was later fitted—Mounting visible.   (R. B. Thorp)

AVRO LANCASTER IN UNIT SERVICE

This is the story of one of the world's greatest fighting planes — the Avro 683 Lancaster.

The Lancaster was developed from a comparative failure, the Avro Manchester, an aircraft with a basically sound airframe, but whose performance was marred by the uncertain performance of its two Rolls Royce Vulture engines.

The Manchester had entered service in limited numbers in late 1940, but by the time the aircraft first operated in February 1941, it had already been realized that the resources and time needed to overcome its engine difficulties were more than could be spared. Britain's war fortunes — Bomber Command's in particular — were at a low ebb and there was a desperate need to carry the war much more to Germany than was possible with existing bombers.

It was decided, therefore, to try out four Merlin X engines in a Manchester, and a momentous decision it proved! The re-equipped machine, BT 308, a triple-finned version, first flew on 9th January, 1941, from Ringway, piloted by H. A. Brown. It was such an obvious success that contracts for the Manchester (which had not yet operated) were immediately revised.

The second prototype, DG 595, with the larger twin fins and more Powerful Merlin XX's, took to the air on May 13th, 1941, also from Ringway, and soon joined BT 308 at A. & A.E.E., Boscombe Down.

Lancaster production, using up Manchester airframes already under construction, started at L 7527.

Entry into service

Development went so smoothly that by the end of 1941, the Lancaster was ready to enter squadron service with No. 44 (Rhodesian) Squadron at Waddington (5 Group). Some experienced 5 Group crews had been detached to Boscombe Down from mid-1941 onwards to gain experience on the Lancaster and to participate in the development flying programme, before helping to convert the squadrons.

Operations

Introduction to operations was delayed by bad weather and training requirements until 3rd March, 1942, when four of 44's Lancasters mined Heligoland Bight, but the first bombing operation was on the night of the 10th March, 1942, when two Lancasters of No. 44 Squadron participated in a raid on Essen.

Following the complete re-equipment of No. 44 Squadron, the next to receive Lancasters was No. 97 (Straits Settlement) Squadron, at Coningsby, also in No. 5 Group. Both squadrons were to have a long association with the Lancaster.

Some structural weaknesses appeared, and in March 1942, R 5539, a new Lancaster, was sent to A. & A.E.E. for diving test trials, during which speeds of 450 m.p.h. were achieved. On its 21st dive, R 5539 became inverted and was lost when the port wing fell off pulling out.

The Lancaster was such a delight to fly, particularly after the Manchester, that many pilots were no doubt unable to resist its fighter-like handling qualities, and aircraft continued to be lost because of operational and design limitations being grossly exceeded.

It was not until after the Augsburg raid of the 17th April, 1942, that the Lancaster was officially announced to the public, though by this time it was anything but a secret to the people of Lincolnshire and Nottinghamshire. The Lancaster and its successor the Lincoln were, in fact, destined to become something of a way of life for them for over fifteen years.

The Augsburg raid, though successful, was to be the first and last major daylight raid by Lancasters for six months because of the disastrous losses. Of the 12 aircraft sent out, 6 from each of No's 44 and 97 Squadrons, only 5 returned safely, including that of the leader of the raid, Sqn/Ldr. J. D. Nettleton, D.F.C., of 44 Squadron, who was awarded the first V.C. on Lancasters.

Until mid 1942 squadrons receiving Lancasters were preoccupied with conversion and training and were playing only a very limited part in the bombing offensive, including the 1,000 bomber raids which took place in May and June.

By this time, most Lancasters carried the first major visible modification — the fairing round the mid upper turret in which was housed the guide rails and cut-outs which prevented the gunner spraying his own aircraft with bullets. The fairing also reduced turbulence and drag.

The need to train more Lancaster crews was becoming increasingly urgent and beyond the capacity of the squadrons, each of which had a Conversion Flight. As newly trained aircrews, with no operational experience, began to appear, more specialized training was obviously needed, the Lancaster being a highly complex — and precious — machine.

In May 1942 the first Conversion Unit, No. 1654, was formed at Swinderby, with Manchesters initially, but receiving Lancasters in June before moving to Wigsley, a satellite airfield. Also using Swinderby at the time was 61 Squadron's Conversion Flight, a typical aircraft being R 5853 QR-E. The " bar " over individual code

BIII PA975, MG–G, 7 Squadron, Oakington, 7/3/45. The red flash denotes Flt/Lt. J. A. McCollah & crew's association with this Lanc on which they did most of their tour of ops. Note earlier small-style codes still visible, as originally used on the Squadron's Stirlings.   (J. A. McCollah)

letters distinguished the aircraft from those of the Squadron operating from nearby Syerston, and was fairly common with Conversion Flights at the time.

The remaining Conversion Flights combined to form No's 1660 and 1661 C.U.'s by the end of October, and before the end of 1942, No. 1 Group, already converting to Lancasters, had formed its own C.U. — No. 1656 — at Lindholme.

The Lancasters issued to Conversion Units (later Heavy Conversion Units — H.C.U.'s) were generally the oldest aircraft on the squadrons, and were fitted with dual controls by means of extension arms to control wheel and rudders from the first pilot's position. Some of the earliest H.C.U. aircraft survived the war, being from the first L., W. and R. serial batches, and this bears remarkable testimony to the durability of the Lancaster, which would probably suffer more at the hands of trainee crews for three years than in six months of operations!

By July 1942, No. 5 Group was wholly re-equipped and the Lancaster soon began to establish itself as the premier weapon of Bomber Command. It was far exceeding expectations as to range, carrying capacity, durability, manoeuverability etc. Its handling qualities and the reduction in percentage losses which it brought about made it popular with crews. In the late summer of 1942 it was operating in some force at night against the vital targets in the Ruhr, and was helping to bring about the badly needed improvement in morale which the nation needed after three years on the receiving end.

In addition to bombing and mining operations, shipping patrols of 8 to 9 hours duration were also undertaken by No's 44, 50 and 61 Squadrons while on detachment to Coastal Command at St. Eval. Some aircraft and crews of No. 44 Squadron were also detached to Gibraltar for the same purpose in July. One of the Lancasters, R 5494, carrying a full load of spares and ground crew, lost an engine 500 miles from Gibraltar, swung on landing at North Front and caught fire, fortunately with no loss of life.

At this time of the war, Bomber Command's techniques were lacking. Losses were heavy and, even though the Lancaster was a vast improvement on older types, many bombs were being wasted. The safest times to operate were in the dirtiest weather, or on moonless nights, but these conditions produced the poorest results. In August 1942 therefore, in an effort to increase effectiveness, No. 8 Group Pathfinder Force was formed, and to it was transferred No. 83 Squadron, from Scampton to Wyton. In replacement No. 5 Group received 57 Squadron from No. 3 Group, Norfolk.

No. 5 Group's squadrons had a busy time in October 1942. On the 17th October, 94 Lancasters took part in a

$10\frac{1}{2}$ hour low-level trip to bomb the Le Creusot Armament Works, deep inside German-occupied territory only 90 miles from Geneva. All aircraft flew in loose formation below 1,000 feet, their roundabout route taking them over Cornwall and the Bay of Biscay before crossing the west coast of France; then across 330 miles of enemy territory to reach the target at sunset. Only one Lancaster was lost.

Italian industrial targets were attacked several times during the last two weeks of October by day and night, Genoa, Turin and Milan all receiving attention.

No. 1 Group was the next to re-equip with Lancasters, beginning in October/November 1942, No's 101 and 460 (Australian) Squadrons being the first to operate them. By the end of 1942 there were fifteen squadrons operating Lancasters, with a total strength nearing 200 aircraft. No. 5 Group had also formed an Australian squadron (No. 467) in November 1942.

Throughout the war, Lancaster squadrons were to have a distinctly international flavour. Not everyone on an Australian or Canadian squadron would be from those two countries, and any one crew on any squadron might have in it men of seven different nationalities, being volunteers from all over the world. Many Americans had, for instance, enlisted in the R.C.A.F. before Pearl Harbour and served operationally on Lancasters.

In the early days of Lancaster operations, a crew comprised two pilots, observer (who did navigation and bombing), two W/Ops. (one of whom would man the front guns), mid-upper and rear gunners, the crews having come mainly from the Manchester. In mid 1942 the second pilot was replaced by a Flight Engineer and the normal crew became seven: pilot, flight engineer, navigator, bomb aimer/front gunner, W/Op., mid-upper and rear gunners. Some specialist squadrons carried an eighth crew member as detailed later, and a ventral gunner was sometimes carried when daylight raids were resumed in 1944.

With the advent of the Lancaster, demand for Merlin engines threatened to outstrip supply, and as a safeguard, the Hercules-engined Lancaster Mk. II appeared. The Lancaster Mark II Trials Flight was formed at Syerston in early November 1942, with three tour-expired pilots, Sqn/Ldr. W. I. Deas, Flt/Lt. J. V. Hopgood (later of Dams Raid fame) and Fg/Off. T. B. Cole.

The first aircraft, DS 603 and DS 605, were tested at various heights, speeds and loads before entering service in 61 Squadrons markings in January 1943. DS 608, QR-0, was the first Mk. II to bomb Germany on 16th January, 1943, being flown to Berlin by Fg/Off. Jack Cockshott. The same aircraft and crew attacked Berlin again the next night.

BI LM211, MG–Z, 7 Squadron, Summer 1945, still bearing red 'Z' outlined in yellow from its previous service in 5 Group as ZN–Z, 106 Squadron.
(T. W. Reynolds)

The Mk. II's on the Trials Flight reached 24,000 feet lightly loaded on test, but with a bomb load struggled to reach 18,000, a disadvantage in the face of increasing night-fighter and flak defences. They were, however, faster than the Merlin-engined Lancasters at lower levels, had a better initial rate of climb, and their air-cooled engines were reliable under fire, being less vulnerable to coolant leaks. Fuel consumption was greater and the Italian targets left little or no margin.

No. 5 Group did not take to the Mk. II; and those from 61 Squadron had all been delivered to 3 Group by the end of February 1943, where they were gratefully received by 115 Squadron at East Wretham, in place of Wellingtons.

1943 was a year of steady conversion from older types of bombers to Lancasters by existing squadrons, and by the formation of new squadrons to absorb expanding deliveries. No. 1 Group, based mainly in North Lincolnshire, converted its last Wellington Squadron, No. 166, reformed No. 100 Squadron, and formed three new squadrons — each with a nucleus from existing squadrons.

No. 3 Group, based in Norfolk and Cambridgeshire, formed a new squadron, 514, in September 1943, to take further deliveries of the Mk. II.

No. 8 (Pathfinder) Group converted two of its squadrons, No's 7 and 156, to Lancasters from Stirlings and Wellingtons, and acquired 97 Squadron from 5 Group for marker duties in April, to join its existing Lancaster Squadron No. 83. No. 405 (Vancouver) Squadron R.C.A.F. also joined No. 8 Group from 6 Group shortly before converting from Halifaxes to Lancasters.

No. 6 (R.C.A.F.) Group was a newcomer to the scene of Lancaster operations in 1943, and converted No's 408 (Goose), 426 (Thunderbird) and 432 (Leaside) Squadrons from Wellingtons and Halifaxes to Lancaster Mk. II's between June and October.

No. 5 Group formed a new squadron late in March 1943, No. 617, initially known as " Squadron X ", whose exploits were to become legendary. Its successful attack on the Mohne, Eder and Sorpe dams on the night of 16/17th May, 1943, earned the squadron the title of " The Dam Busters ". The story of the attack, surely one of the most daring precision bombing raids of all time, is so well known as to make it beyond the scope of this book. The ingenious modifications to the 19 Lancaster Mk. III's used have now been well publicized. Wing Commander Guy Gibson won the V.C. for his leadership of the raid, in which eight aircraft were lost.

As the dams raid was to be carried out at exceptionally low level, consideration was given by " higher authority " to the use of Lancaster Mk. II's, in view of their slight superiority in speed. The idea was resisted strongly by the senior crews, and in particular by one of the squadron's pilots, " Hoppy " Hopgood, who had some experience on the Mk. II's of the Syerston Trials Flight. Shortage of time was also an important factor.

All the special aircraft had a /G serial suffix, which appear to have been deleted for the operation itself. Some of them survived the war, being converted to carry 12,000 lb. bombs. Guy Gibson's aircraft on the dams raid, ED 932, AJ-G became AJ-V, and operated with the

squadron from Coningsby until at least January 1944. Normal loads were either a 12,000 lb. light-case blast bomb, or $14 \times 1,000$ lb. bombs, and eventually the 12,000 lb Tallboy.

No. 617 Squadron remained in No. 5 Group until the end of the war as a specialist precision bombing unit, doing its own target marking, firstly in Lancasters then in Mosquitos and Mustangs, the techniques being developed by Wg/Cdr. Leonard Cheshire, V.C., D.S.O., D.F.C. It was a volunteer squadron, most of its aircrews having already completed, or nearly so, a tour of operations and who wished to continue without spending the normal rest period instructing at an H.C.U. or O.T.U.

1943 was the year the offensive against the German industrial cities — the Battle of the Ruhr — really got under way. Bombing effectiveness was increased by better marking techniques and by blind bombing aids such as H2S, which was first used operationally by 49 Squadron in August. No. 8 Group (P.F.F.) were early adopters and on its H2S aircraft the bomb aimer became known as a " Nav. II " to operate the set. For some time all H2S aircraft carried a /G serial suffix, which denoted that secret equipment was aboard. It was also applied to those aircraft of 101 Squadron which, from October 1943, were equipped with " ABC " radio/radar counter-measures equipment, and which carried an additional W/Op. who could transmit false messages in German.

Such was the intensity of the campaign against the Ruhr, that a crew could complete a tour of 30 operations in under six months in mid-1943 if they were lucky enough to survive. German defences were constantly improved and increased, and heavy losses were inflicted on the bomber force which was now becoming predominantly Lancaster.

A trip to the Ruhr would normally take 4 to 6 hours, depending on routing, winds, load, height; those to more eastern targets such as Munich, Berlin, etc., would be of 7 to 9 hours duration, calling for considerable reserves of stamina by pilots and crew, at height levels up to 23,000 feet, using unsophisticated autopilots, oxygen and heating equipment. Gunners would sometimes suffer badly from exposure on the coldest nights, the rear gunner in particular who, with the centre panel of his turret removed, was open to the elements. The Lancaster, unlike its American counterparts, the B-17 and B-29, was not built for comfort. There were no ash trays or sound proofing, and the four Merlin's were not the quietest of engines. This latter feature in itself was said to give the crews " Dutch courage ", as they could not hear the hell that was being let loose outside.

On 17/18th August, 1943, the rocket research establishment at Peenemunde was destroyed. This was the night, with Lancasters forming a sizeable proportion of the 600-strong force, that the Master Bomber technique was used for the first time on a large scale. Its potential had been realized following the Dams Raid, when Guy Gibson had directed his attackers by V.H.F. The technique had, in fact, been used before, on the night of 2nd December, 1942, when Sqn/Ldr. S. Pat Daniels broadcast to the main force by R/T over Frankfurt from his Lancaster I, R5754, OL-K, of 83 Squadron.

By the end of 1943, with the Battle of Berlin under

Bl PD211, WS–M, 9 Squadron, Bardney. Crash-landed at Belomorsk, Russia, 12/9/44 on the Tirpitz operation "Paravane". After a 12-hour flight, the intended Russian airfield of Yagodnik could not be found due to bad weather, and the skipper, Flt/Lt. G. C. Camsell, RCAF, put down on a wooden-planked landing strip on the edge of a small town. Codes—red, outlined in yellow, as adopted by 5 Group Autumn 1944. Codes repeated on upper and lower surfaces of tailplanes. Dorsal turret removed & Wellington overload petrol tank installed. Bomb load—a 12,000lb "Tallboy". (H. R. Humphries)

Above: BI W4366, PH–R, 12 Squadron, Wickenby, circa 3/43. Flt/Lt. J. O. Lancaster's kite. This squadron was unique in displaying all its codes aft of the roundels until late 1943. Note that serial no. has been erased from normal fuselage position, and put above tailplane. Some Lancs of the squadron had code and identity letters reversed.

(J. O. Lancaster)

Above: BIII ED993, PH–J, 12 Squadron, Wickenby, circa 5/43. Close up showing codes on starboard side and the erased serial number. Sitting in the doorway is Sgt. P. D. Baxter, Flight Engineer to Sqn/Ldr. F. B. Slade. O.C. 'A' Flight. (P. D. Baxter)

way, the number of squadrons using the Lancaster had increased to 35, and in total some 600 aircraft which, towards the year's close, were being supplemented by the first Canadian built Mk. X's with Packard Merlins, nearly all of which went to Canadian squadrons.

The Packard-Merlined Mk. III had also been delivered in considerable numbers since the beginning of the year, and the Mk's I and III were to be produced concurrently until the end of the war. The engines were the only difference between the aircraft, performances being almost identical, though the American carburration system was the better one and gave the aircraft a slightly more economical cruising rate. The engines themselves were interchangeable and a Mk. I could become a Mk. III and vice-versa on engine changes. Some aircraft flew with both British and American Merlins fitted together. Hamilton propellers (broad blades), which originated from the Packard-built engines, were gradually fitted to most aircraft, giving improved take-off, climb and ceiling. Aircraft so equipped became known to the crews as "paddle steamers".

The idea that the Mk. III was a development of the Mk. I is a popular misconception.

The H.C.U's had also expanded to keep pace with the increasing number of squadrons. No. 3 Group formed 1678 Mk. II Con. Flt. (later Con. Unit) from 115 Squadron's Con. Flight in much the same way as No. 5 Group's C.U's had been formed in 1942. By late autumn of 1943, No. 8 Group (P.F.F.) had also formed its own conversion unit, known as The Navigational Training Unit (N.T.U.).

Conversion Units occasionally sent aircraft on raids (diversionary usually), a new crew flying under the captaincy of an instructor with at least one tour of operations behind him.

Later in the year, the H.C.U's began to lose most of their Lancasters for Halifaxes and Stirlings, on which crews could gain 4-engined experience before passing to the newly-formed Lancaster Finishing Schools for a final short conversion to the Lancaster, thus conserving vital Lancaster flying hours. No's 1 and 5 Groups each formed an L.F.S. in November 1943 from flights of the Conversion Units. No. 3 Group's L.F.S. followed in December 1943. No. 6 L.F.S., however, was not formed until December 1944 and was used not by 6 Group but by Transport Command and B.O.A.C. to train pilots for the Lancastrian.

1944 was the year in which the Lancaster emerged supreme, with 20 more squadrons being either newly-formed or converting from other types. No. 3 Group by the end of the year had become virtually all Lancaster. Four of the Canadian squadrons in 6 Group converted from Halifaxes, 8 Group (P.F.F.) formed two new

squadrons and No. 3 Group changed its Mk. II's for Merlin-engined variants. During the year No. 6 Group's three Canadian squadrons gave up their Lancaster Mk. II's for Halifaxes, as Mk. II production had ended by March 1944 and operational life of existing machines was running out.

The main force would now invariably be mainly Lancaster, supported by Halifaxes. Attacks on German industrial targets continued, but in addition, the softening-up in preparation for D-Day began, railways, marshalling yards, canals, ports in France and the Low Countries receiving close attention.

In the early hours of D-Day, 6th June, 1944, 617's Lancasters carried out a precision low level exercise to fool the enemy radar into thinking a large force of invasion ships was on its way across the Channel much further north than was the case, and No. 101 Squadron put up 21 aircraft for "jamming" enemy radar.

Following D-Day, attacks were made on enemy troop concentrations and supply lines. Daylight raids were resumed, often with fighter escorts, and the V-bomb sites were attacked intensively until September.

On 8th June, 1944, 617 Squadron's Lancasters dropped the first 12,000 lb. "Tallboy" bombs, wrecking a railway tunnel. Over 850 Tallboys were to be dropped before the war ended. The aircraft had specially bulged bomb bays, similar to those of the Mk. II Lancaster, but the bomb doors did not quite close with the load aboard. Many of No. 9 Squadron's Lancasters at Bardney were also equipped to carry the Tallboy and usually accompanied No. 617 on operations, including the three attacks on the Tirpitz, which was finally capsized in November 1944.

In March 1945, 617 Squadron, using Lancaster B.1 (Specials) with cut-away bomb bays, dropped the first 22,000 lb. (10-ton) "Grand Slams", designed by Barnes Wallis, who had also been responsible for the Dams bomb and the "Tallboys". They had more powerful Merlins and, as they operated only in daylight, exhaust

BI NG358, LS–H, 15 Squadron, Mildenhall, mid 1945. Note yellow bars on the fins to denote G–H formation leader and also the mustard coloured gas detection 'patch' forward of the dorsal turret. (G. A. Pound)

shrouds were removed. They also had stronger under-carriages known as the "Mk. IV", designed for the Lincoln which was at first designated the Lancaster IV.

Daylight raids in 1944/45 led to the re-appearance of ventral guns, usually fitted on squadron initiative. Early Lancasters had been fitted with two Browning .303's aft of the bomb bay, but they had been removed for night operations. The later guns were twin or single 0.5's or a single 20 mm. cannon firing through a hole in the floor. No. 3 Group particularly favoured ventral guns and for daylight raids most of its squadrons would have three or four aircraft so equipped.

Another "squadron mod." had been by No's 7 and 97 who had decided in early 1944 that the front turret was superfluous and had faired many of their's over, ex-amples being ND496 MG:T and ND346 OF:O. The turrets were hurriedly replaced for daylight operations, German fighters quickly discovering the aircrafts' vul-nerability to head-on attacks.

The Rose-Rice rear turret, with $2 \times .5$'s appeared in some aircraft of 1 Group, its squadrons being the nearest to Gainsborough where the turrets were made. No. 101 Squadron, most of whose aircraft also carried the "Air-borne Cigar" radio-jamming devices, were first users of these turrets, closely followed by 166.

From the autumn of 1944 a small number of Lan-casters were fitted with A.G.L.(T), a radar-controlled rear turret. 49 Squadron was the pioneer, followed by 635, 156 and 101, but the turrets were troublesome, and were not persevered with, in spite of further trials from September 1945 by 115 Squadron, using aircraft from 49 Squadron.

An interesting development took place in No. 1 Group, whose speciality was bombing marshalling yards, am-munition dumps, etc. The group formed its own Special Duties Flight at Binbrook for target marking in April 1944, under the command of Sqn/Ldr. H. F. Breakspear from 100 Squadron. Squadrons in the group provided two experienced crews, who took their own aircraft with them, still bearing their parent squadron's codes. On attachment to the S.D.F., large white bands were crudely painted on fins and rudders and "squared" code letters alloted to differentiate between 460 Squadron's aircraft over the R/T; examples were ND 863 - CF:0² (625

Squadron) and ME 648 - HW:R² (100 Squadron). The S.D.F. was short lived, closing down in July 1944 due to "outside pressures". The crews and aircraft returned to their original squadrons, where new codes were issued and the "squared" dropped.

From early 1945 onwards, most of the Canadian 6 Group Squadrons still operating Halifaxes had converted to Lancasters (Mark X in the main). Strangely enough, the three which had used Lancaster II's in 1943, No's 408, 426 and 432, had converted to Halifaxes in 1944 and received their Lancaster X's too late to operate them.

By the end of the war, there were 54 squadrons operat-ing Lancasters, with 745 in front line use and 296 in training units. Many squadrons had three flights, an example being 149 who had A and B Flights coded OJ and C Flight TK. Other squadrons with more aircraft than alphabet letters would designate a flight with a "Bar" above the aircraft's individual letter, or use a "squared" letter. This latter method was also used by No. 1 Group to distinguish between two different squadrons using the same airfield, e.g. 12 and 626 at Wickenby. The former's aircraft had standard codes, while those of the latter were "squared", such as UM - Y², ME 584.

In three years of operations, Lancasters dropped 608,613 tons of bombs, 63.8% of Bomber Command's total, in 156,318 sorties. Approximately 3,800 were lost, all but 10% in action.

7,377 were built by the Lancaster Production Group, comprising six companies.

Post war

Immediate tasks were supply dropping to the Dutch (operation MANNA), P.O.W. repatriation from Brussels (operation EXODUS), and repatriation of allied soldiers from Bari in Italy (operation DODGE in the autumn of 1945). At one time, over 100 Lancasters were stranded at Bari due to bad weather.

When the European war finished, plans had already been made for Lancasters (and Lincolns) to operate against Japan — "Tiger Force". The Lancaster-equipped Canadian squadrons returned home to prepare, and in England, squadrons of No.'s 3 and 5 Groups were to be

BI L7537, KM–L, 44 (Rhodesia) Squadron, Waddington, 1/42—the first Lanc de-livered to a squadron. Note grey codes, standard in Bomber Command at the time, fin flash of equal partitions, and dorsal turret without fairing. It is not known whether the identity letter "L" was coinci-dental or intentional,—i.e. "L" for Lancaster. (H. R. Humphries)

BIII ME308/G, EA–F, 49 Squadron, Fulbeck, 11/44. Fg/Off. C. C. Watson's kite. Just discernable is the A.G.L.(T) which the squadron pioneered on service trials.
(C. C. Watson)

this country's contribution. The atomic bomb, and Japan's subsequent early surrender, put an end to Tiger Force, which was disbanded in October 1945. Shortly afterwards, deliveries of Lancasters specially modified for use in the Far East were begun. The aircraft, all either Mk's I or VII, had tropicalized engines, and were designated F/E (Far East).

The British built Merlin T24, incorporating the American-type carburration system was decided upon for the post war bomber force because of its slightly higher reliability factor, better overload boost duration, and less tendency to overheat than the Packard-built Merlins.

Apart from their mid upper turret, Mks. I (F/E) and VII (F/E) were virtually identical, all having FN 82 rear turrets with 2 × .5's; some had bulged bomb bays, a feature of late production I's and III's.

From November 1945 to April 1947 three Middle East Squadrons were re-equipped with Lancaster I (F/E) and VII (F/E) to replace Lease-Lend Liberators. Their flying consisted mainly of training sorties, patrols of the Canal Zone, mail carrying, and ferrying female service personnel to and from weekend dances!

The majority of the wartime Lancaster squadrons were quickly disbanded after Japan's capitulation and the remaining Lancaster squadrons re-grouped. By the autumn of 1945 the Lincoln was beginning to appear, No. 57 Squadron being the first to receive them in August 1945 for trials. Re-equipment with the Lincoln really got under way in the summer of 1946, 10 former Lancaster squadrons having converted by the end of the year (8 of them from the old 5 Group, which had disappeared in the post war reorganisation). The withdrawal of the Lancaster continued until the spring of 1950, when 49 Squadron — one of the first with Lancasters in 1942 — converted to Lincolns. So ended almost eight years of distinguished service as a front line bomber.

One Bomber Command unit operated Lancasters until 15th December, 1953. This was 82 Squadron, which used specially modified Lancaster PR.I's for aerial survey and photographic work. The squadron started life as the Radio Controlled Air Survey Unit, using Mosquitos and crews from Max Aitken's Banff Wing. The large camera magazines could not be changed in the confines of a Mosquito, so a change to Lancasters was made. No. 541 Squadron was quickly formed at Benson, and Flt/Lt. Turner-Hughes, an Armstrong Whitworth Test Pilot, was called in to give the pilots a quick conversion. Quick it was too! After only 1¼ hours dual, Flt/Lt. Phil Kilmister, D.F.C., A.F.C., went solo, with his usual Mosquito observer, Fg/Off. Alf Lloyd acting as Engineer, neither having any previous 4-engined experience. The squadron flew out to Africa in March 1946. In October 1946, No. 82 Squadron re-formed from a Flight of 541 at Yundum (Accra), and for a time the two squadrons operated together. No. 541 disbanded, leaving No. 82 to carry on the survey which, until October 1952, covered over 1½ million square miles. One of 82 Squadron's aircraft was PA 474, the R.A.F.'s sole surviving Lancaster in flying condition at the time of writing (1969). Its last Lancaster, PA 427 — the last in Bomber Command — was withdrawn in December 1953.

COASTAL COMMAND decided upon the Lancaster as a replacement for Lease-Lend Liberators and Hudsons.

As early as November 1944, A.S.W.D.U. had formed a trials detachment at Coningsby, with tour-expired Bomber Command crews, using Lancasters PB 801, PB 803, PB 809 and PB 810, all Mk. I's, though the Mk. III was subsequently used almost exclusively. These aircraft were test-flown by Flt/Lt. Frank Thomas, D.F.C., and crew of 54 Base, one of 5 Group's centralised servicing units, which, based at Coningsby, overhauled aircraft from No's 83, 106, 617 and 97 Squadrons.

Late in 1945 the first ASR III, RF 310, complete with airborne lifeboat, was sent to 279 Squadron, Thornaby, along with five others. The squadron, operating the Warwick and Walrus, formed a Lancaster Flight, which was sent out to Burma as 1348 Flight (coded RL) to supplement, and then replace Lease-Lend Liberators. All the pilots and co-pilots were from 514 Squadron, Bomber Command, the navigators and W/Ops. being ex Coastal Command C.O. was Sqn/Ldr. A. C. Barden.

No. 1348 Flight was withdrawn to the Middle East in May 1946 and lost its identity in a rapid and complicated reorganisation of units, out of which emerged No's 37 and 38 Squadrons, still using the code RL, which had now been used by six units.

Eventually, No's 37 and 38 operated jointly in Malta, both using the code RL; 37's aircraft using the first half of the alphabet, and 38's the second half. No. 38 Squadron was the last front line R.A.F. unit to use the Lancaster, the last one, RF 273, leaving Malta on 3rd February, 1954.

Towards the end of its stay in Malta, and following 37 Squadron's withdrawal, No. 38 dropped the code RL and reverted to single code letters.

The home-based Coastal Lancasters were used by 224 (45/46 only), 203 and 210 Squadrons at St. Eval (1945/46) and 120 at Leuchars and Kinloss, which also housed No. 236 O.C.U. (formerly 6 O.T.U.). Lancasters continued with these units until 1951/53 when they were replaced with Neptunes and Shackletons.

The Lancaster ASR 3 became the GR 3 with rear-camera mounting etc., and ultimately, the MR 3, with Lincoln undercarriage and rudders, and improved radar and sonar equipment. The ASR 3 had formerly been the ASR III but was redesignated like all other aircraft, in 1950, when the R.A.F. adopted Arabic in place of Roman numerals.

Airborne lifeboats continued to be carried until 1953, but they were always troublesome. The boats were designed to fit flush against the Lancaster's closed bomb doors, and were clamped to a tubular metal fitting projecting from the bomb-bay roof through a hole in the bomb doors. Earlier lifeboats had a small door in the side, so that when being winched up, a man — usually the smallest available — could stay in the boat to see that it was properly secured. Later, inspection hatches were provided in the aircraft floor.

On withdrawal from the squadrons, the remaining MR 3's were allotted to No. 1 School of Maritime Reconnaissance at St. Mawgan (formerly 236 O.C.U.) where they were used to train Shackleton crews, until 15th October, 1956, when RF 325 — the last Lancaster in R.A.F. service — was withdrawn for scrapping, thus ending an R.A.F. unit connection of fifteen years.

Lancaster 7, NX 739, survived in Ministry of Supply photography service at Blackbushe until January 1957, and PR 1 PA 474 flew on laminar-flow wing trials until

1964, still in its 82 Squadron markings. It was adopted by R.A.F. Waddington and still flies.

The Lancaster served with many other specialist units until the early 1950's, and was used to test a variety of engines and equipment.

Although the Lancastrian was the civil development, some Lancasters were used by civil airlines for mail carrying and crew training. Flight Refuelling modified a number as airborne tankers, firstly for use with "Tiger Force", then for refuelling non-stop transAtlantic aircraft. They also served in the 1948 Berlin air lift.

THE ARGENTINE AIR FORCE took delivery of 15 Lancaster B Mk. 1's in 1948, coded B-031 to 045. They were almost new aircraft, brought out of storage and were standard R.A.F. B.1's. The pilots were converted and checked out at Langar by Peter J. Field-Richards, the resident AVRO test pilot. The aircraft were based at Villa Mercedes, Rio Quarto and the Paratroop Training School, Cordoba. Few bombs and little ammunition were available but the Lancasters were in minor action in some of the country's revolutions in the late 1950's. Their main task, however, was long-range transport flights in support of polar expeditions, and patrols along the thousands of miles of borders with Chile and Bolivia to prevent cattle and drug smuggling.

Some are known to have been lost in the Andes, but it has not been disclosed how many survive. By the early 1960's, spares were known to be a problem but it is possible that one or two Lancasters may still be active at the time of writing.

THE ROYAL EGYPTIAN AIR FORCE took delivery of nine Lancaster B. Mk. 1's coded 1801-1809 in Arabic. Like those supplied to Argentina, the almost-new aircraft were taken from store and were standard B 1's throughout, with turrets, but without guns, bullets or bombs. Though some Egyptian aircrew were trained at Woodford, few of them flew the Lancasters, which were based at Almaza. AVRO's lent two technicians, Messrs. A. W. Dale (airframes) and E. Griffiths (electrics), who stayed for a year. In that time, each Lancaster was flown once a month only by a Rolls Royce pilot, Andrew MacDowell.

It is not known whether any Lancasters survive in Egypt though some were reported as being seen on the ground during the 1956 Suez campaign. It is more than likely that, with no spares available, they never operated and were left to decay in the sand at Almaza.

No additional markings are known to have been applied

and it is doubtful if, in the desert atmosphere, a repaint was ever needed. The light/medium sea grey in which the upper surfaces were finished soon became bleached a sandy grey, the colour which AVRO's had suggested originally.

THE FRENCH NAVY (L'Aeronavale) took delivery of 54 Lancasters (32 Mk. 1's and 22 Mk. 7's) in 1952 at a cost of £50,000 each, under N.A.T.O. defence plans. Hence the codes WU (Western Union).

The Lancasters, built in 1945, were taken from store and brought virtually up to R.A.F. MR standard at Langar and Woodford, including airborne lifeboat fittings.

Crews were trained at R.A.F. St. Eval, and the aircraft were based along the coasts of North Africa and S.W. France, doing sterling service until withdrawn from 1955/61.

A number, however, continued to serve with Escadrille de Servitude 9's at Noumea in the South Pacific on maritime reconnaissance duties. The aircraft were regular visitors to Australia and New Zealand before finally retiring in 1964. The original trio were WU 16, 27 and 41, which were eventually replaced by WU 13, 15 and 21. Three are preserved, WU 13 (NX 665) in New Zealand, WU 16 (NX 622) in Australia and WU 15 (NX 611) which was flown from Australia to the United Kingdom in May 1965.

FRENCH (CIVIL). Five Lancaster 7's were delivered from 1953/54 for use with the French equivalent of the British Coast Guard. The aircraft were up to MR standard, with Mk. 4 undercarriages and Lincoln-type rudders. They were based at Maison Blanche (Algeria) and Agadir (Morocco) for patrol duties and air sea rescue work and flown by French Navy crews.

THE ROYAL CANADIAN AIR FORCE was a large post-war user of the Canadian built Mk. 10. The pattern aircraft, R 5727, complete with ventral guns, had arrived in Toronto in August 1942, and by 1945, 430 were built. All had Packard Merlin's, and Hamilton airscrews. Some had Martin mid-upper turrets fitted post-war as in the Lancaster 7.

Unlike the British (F/E) marks, and the Egyptian Lancasters, the main problem in Canada was the cold in which the aircraft would be required to operate. KB 739, KB 954 and FM 148 were subjected to rigorous cold-weather trials from 1946 to 1950 at the Winter Experimental Establishment, as a result of which, Lancasters were cleared, with certain minor modifications, to

Right: BIII DV156, VN–C, 50 Squadron. Skellingthorpe. Here seen at Blida. North Africa. after the "Shuttle" raid on Friedrichshaven 20/21 June, 1943. Plt/Off. J. Mason's kite. Note size of identity letter.
(D. Grant)

Below: BI W4357, QR–A, 61 Squadron. Syerston, 4–6/43. Sgt. M. C. Lowe's kite. The airfield is visible in the background, 'A—Apple's' dispersal being situated on the south side of the main Leicester—Newark road. (M. C. Lowe)

BI or BIII AA–F of 75 (New Zealand) Squadron, Mepal, early 1945, taxies out for a raid on Kiel. G–H equipped. (J. Hunt)

operate in temperatures of −40°C. At −51°C, the perspex canopies cracked.

Canadian Lancasters were so extensively modified, they became known to Avro Canada's staff as "the flying mods". Designations included:—

10 MR	(Maritime Reconnaissance)
10 P	(Photographic)
10 N	(Navigation)
10 U	(Unmodified)
10 SR	(Search and Rescue)
10 MP	(Maritime Patrol)
10 S	(Standard)
10 BR	(Bomber Reconnaissance)
10 AR	(Aerial Reconnaissance)

plus odd experimentals.

The variety of duties included mercy missions in the frozen wastes, and over 3½ million square miles of north country was mosaically photographed by 408 and 413 (Photographic) Squadrons. Four Lancasters were continually employed from early spring to late fall to report the movement of arctic ice for shipping forecasts.

Replacement of Lancasters started in the mid 1950's with the arrival of the Neptune, but they continued in service until 1st April, 1964, when 408's last three were withdrawn. Nine Lancasters are preserved in Canada.

NOTES

Colour Views

Unless otherwise stated all insignia depicted appeared on port side only, and all two letter codes appeared on starboard sides aft of the roundels (i.e. standard presentation).

Crews

Where a pilot is named, he is R.A.F. or R.A.F.V.R. unless otherwise specified.

Abbreviations

A. & A.E.E.	Aircraft and Armament Experimental Establishment
A.G.L.(T.)	Automatic Gun Laying (Turret)
A.S.W.D.U.	Air Sea Warfare Development Unit
A.S.R.	Air Sea Rescue
G.R.	General Reconnaissance
M.R.	Maritime Reconnaissance
O.C.U.	Operational Conversion Unit
O.T.U.	Operational Training Unit
P.F.F.	Pathfinder Force.

Below 2 pictures: BI HK563, JN–W, "Paper Doll", of 'C' Flight, 75 (New Zealand) Squadron, Mepal, circa, 8–11/44, flown by Fg/Off. E. Robertson (RNZAF) and crew. Note bulged bomb-bay and reversed code/identity presentation (port side only) a feature of this squadron. (P. J. Smith)

Below: BIII ME527/G, OL–C, 83 Squadron, Coningsby, Spring 1945, flown by Flt/Lt. M. J. Cassidy RAAF & crew. The yellow-outlined codes are smaller than those of most 5 Group squadrons. No. 83's sister-squadron at Coningsby (97) was similarly marked and both carried codes on tailplanes after their return from 8 Group to 5 Group. (F. E. Harper)

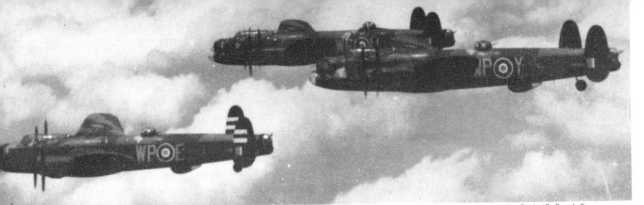

Above: 3 Lancs from 90 Squadron, Tuddenham on a G–H exercise, Spring 1945. Note non-standard 0·5" gun rear turrets. Both 'E–Easy' & 'Y–Yorker' have their dorsal turrets moved forward as on the BVII. Several squadrons carried out their own modifications, pending the arrival of the BVII. (T. W. H. Saunders)

BI NF983, SR–D, 101 Squadron, Ludford Magna, 9–11/44. Flt/Lt. M. C. C. Haycraft's aircraft Note the two aerials for A.B.C. "Airborne Cigar" equipment. Also noteworthy is the Rose-Rice tail turret. Most of 101's Lancs carried the codes forward of the roundels on the starboard side. (M. C. C. Haycraft)

Right: Close up of Rose-Rice tail turret with Flt/Lt. M. C. C. Haycraft posing in front. (M. C. C. Haycraft)

Above: BIII JA963, OF–Q, 97 (Straits Settlements) Squadron, Bourn, 8–11/43. Flt/Lt. D. I. Jones and crew pose for a picture on a sunny afternoon, on which the fuselage windows stand out. Windows were deleted from production Lancs around this period. Squadron had recently been transferred to 8 Group (P.F.F.) (J. L. Hannah)

Right: ZN–K, 106 Squadron, Metheringham, Summer 1944, with dull maroon fin and rudder for daylight ops. Both 1 and 5 Groups' squadrons adopted tail markings post D-Day, and 1 Group extended them to wing-tips. That shown is but one of several used by 106 Squadron. The disc forward of the door remains a mystery as does the identity of the air and ground crews. (R. MacIntosh)

Above: BIII ED905, PM–X, 'C' Flight, 103 Squadron, Elsham Wolds, 5/43, flown by Flt/Lt. F. V. P. Van Rolleghem, a Belgian. He is seen in cockpit in photo right. The two flags are the Belgian National and Union Jack. The ice cream cornet in the row of bomb motifs denotes a raid on Italy.   (F. V. P. Van Rolleghem)

Below: The same Aircraft when with 550 Squadron, North Killingholme, late 1944, now flown by Flt/Lt. D. A. Shaw and crew. Note—new insignia (motto "Ad Extremum") and "Press on Regardless" added above the bombs, which have also been altered. ED905 joined the elite club of 100 'op' veterans when Flt/Lt. Shaw took it to Dusseldorf 2-3/11/44. Early-type pitot head, and port-side cockpit blister retained.
(D. A. Shaw)

Right: ED905 after transfer to 166 Squadron. Kirmington, which formed from 103's 'C' Flight, 9/43. Now coded AS–X and taken over by Sqn/Ldr. B. Pape.   (B. Pape)

Below: 3 Lancs from 138 Squadron, Circa 4/45. 138 gave up it's special duties operations and joined 3 Group in March 1945, moving from Tempsford to Tuddenham. Note that AC–X has it's dorsal turret moved forward and is one of several BI (BVII interim) Lancs issued to the squadron. Far aircraft has yet to receive its codes.   (T. C. Murray)

Above: BII DS620, KO–W, 'B' Flight, 115 Squadron, East Wretham, circa 7/43 & flown by Plt/Off. K. Eggleston & crew. Note shape of bulged bomb bay doors.   (H. Smith)

Below: The same Lanc pictured some time later (possibly at Witchford) & showing an impressive number of completed operational trips. (A. E. Billson)

Right & below: BIII ND758, A4–A, "The Bad Penny", 'C' Flight, 115 Squadron, witchford, circa 7/44. Flown by Fg/Off. D. S. McKechnie (RCAF) and crew. This form of code presentation was unique and was carried on by 195 Squadron, which formed from 115's 'C' Flight.   (F. R. Leatherdale)

Right & below: BI W4851, GT–E, 156 Squadron (PFF), Warboys, 4/43. Flown by Flt/Lt. R. S. D. Kearns, RNZAF and crew and sporting their usual "Saint" insignia. "Daves Dive" appears under the cockpit window.   (R. S. D. Kearns)

Above: BI PD284, OJ–N, 'B' Flight, 149 Squadron (East India), Methwold, Spring 1945. Flown by Flt/Lt. R. C. Shuster and crew.   (F. D. Wolfson)

Left: The nose of the same Lanc.   (F. D. Wolfson)

Below: BI HK795, TK–B, 'C' Flight, 149 (East India) Squadron, Methwold, Spring 1945, with bulged bomb-bay, ventral gun position (common to most 'C' Flight Lancs) and G–H bars. Flown by Flt/Lt. V. H. Gregory and crew.   (V. H. Gregory)

Right: BI NG146, XY–E, 186 Squadron, Tuddenham, 11/44, clearly showing the absence of the central perspex panel in the rear turret to give the rear gunner better vision.
(S. J. Farrington)

Above: A4–P, 195 Squadron, Wratting Common, dropping surplus stocks of incendiaries in the North Sea, June 1945 (operation "Wastage"). See photo of 115 Squadron for notes on code style. (D. H. Davies)

Above: BIII RF199, TC–J2, 170 Squadron, Hemswell, 1945. Flown by Flt/Lt. J. O. Delaney and crew. Two squadrons shared Hemswell (the other being No. 150) and 170's Lancs carried "Squared" letters for easy identification over the R/T. (J. O. Delaney)

Left: Nose of RF199. (J. O. Delaney)

Right: BI PA280, 9J–P, 227 Squadron, Balderton, early 1945. The squadron's C.O. Wg/Cdr. D. M. Balme with his crew. Note white-painted fin for daylight 'ops' and codes outlined in yellow; also cabin air intake above wing, a feature of later production machines. (D. S. Richardson)

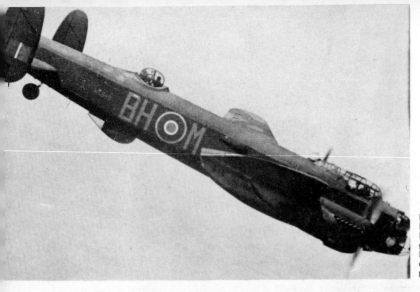

Left: BIII ME549, BH–M, 300 (Masovian) Squadron, Faldingworth, 1945. 300 was unique in being the only Polish Lanc squadron. On the nose is the standard gas disc which appeared on 1 Group's Lancs in 1944. Most of the squadron's aircraft carried a small replica of the Polish Air Force insignia on their noses (usually port side) (W. B. Garnowski)

Above: BI LM257, HA–P, 218 (Gold Coast) Squadron, Chedburgh. Fg/Off. R. G. Walker taking off for Oberhausen 4/12/44, the last 'Op' of his tour. (R. G. Walker)

Below: BX VR–J, of 419 ("Moose") Squadron, RCAF Middleton St. George, 1944. Possibly one of the Squadron's first Lancs. Note bulged bomb bay, a feature of many BX's.
(Canadian Forces Photos)

Right & Below: BX KB864, NA–S, "Sugar's Blues", 428 ("Ghost") Squadron, RCAF, pictured at Malton, Canada, June 1945 when the squadron arrived home from Middleton St. George. Each 'op' is denoted by a girl diving.   (J. E. Goldsmith & Canadian Forces Photos)

Below: BIII JB607, AR–N, 460 Squadron, RAAF, Binbrook 11–12/43. The wartime censor has all but erased the H2S radar blister.   (F. E. Harper)

Below: BI UV–0, 460 Squadron, RAAF, Breighton, Spring 1943, bearing the squadron's original code letters.   (L. J. Simpson)

Above: BI RF175, JO–D, 463 Squadron, RAAF, Waddington, seen at Juvincourt. May 1945. on POW repatriation ("Exodus"). Codes are red outlined in yellow. The identity letter was carried on the fin by several 5 Group squadrons. Note chalked slogans and previous code (VN–50 Squadron) still visible. Serial no. placed higher than usual, to clear the newly-installed static vent, which appears as a white spot. (G. S. Shorthouse)

Above: BIII ND729, PO–L ("Horatio"), 467 Squadron, RAAF, Waddington, Circa 5/44. Note small "PO" on nose: a feature on both the Australian squadrons at Waddington.   (J. Herkes)
Below: BIII PB423, JI–J, 514 Squadron, Waterbeach, Autumn/44. The rear turret is turned almost to its fullest extent towards the camera aircraft.   (P. J. Smith)

Below: Two Lancs from 622 Squadron, Mildenhall, early 1945. GI–K's yellow fin bars have either faded, or been painted over, indicating G–H equipment removed or U/S. The effect of exhaust is clearly seen.   (L. T. Johnson)

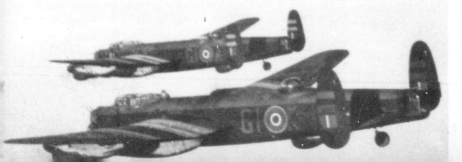

Above: BI PB935, F2–Z, 635 Squadron, Downham Market, at Lubeck 10/5/45 on "Exodus", bringing back former P.O.W.'s. Pilot was Flt/Lt. R. H. Hardy. This squadron's Lancs were equipped at this time with A.G.L.(T.) visible on the aircraft in front.
(Imperial War Museum)

Right: Close up of A.G.L.(T.) on a 635 Squadron Lanc. (R. H. Hardy)

Below: BIII ND931, 60–H, 582 Squadron, (P.F.F.) Little Staughton Taken from a Mosquito of 1409 (Met) Flight piloted by Sqn/Ldr. N Bicknell, 14/7/44, at 15,500 feet. The 'G' suffix has been erased as has the original roundel which was in a non-standard position.
(J. A. L. Currie)

Above: BI (Special) YZ–0, 617 Squadron, Woodhall Spa, 1945 (believed to be PD129). Note the identity letter on the nose fairing and also the codes on the tailplane. At the time of the photograph the '0' had yet to be painted on the starboard tailplane. All codes were red outlined in yellow. The first few BI (Special) Lancs were in standard 'Night' finish but most appeared in 'Day' finish as shown.   (R. M. Horsley)

Above & Left: BI DV385, KC–A "Thumper Mk III." 617 Squadron, Woodhall Spa, mid 1944, flown by Flt/Lt. R. H. Knights and crew. Note bulged bomb bay. On the nose close up D-Day is denoted by a "D" on a bomb symbol while a swastika on bomb No. 32 indicates a fighter destroyed.   (N. R. Ross, & E. Twells)

Below: BIII (Special) ED886, AJ–0, 617 Squadron, Scampton, flown by F/S. W. C. Townsend on the Dams raid of 16/17 May 1943. The fitting for the ventral gun (removed for the raid) is visible, aft of the bomb bay.   (617 Squadron)

Right & below: BIII PB150, CF–V, 625 Squadron, Scampton, circa 6/45. Another member of the "100 club", though the last 7 ops were food drops to the starving Dutch people (Operation "Manna" officially, but "Spam" to the crews). The trips counted as 'ops' due to the uncertainty of the truce arranged at the time with the Germans. Note the 1 Group gas disc. This aircraft was V, V^2 and V again during its service with the squadron. (R. C. Fentiman)

Left: A Lanc over Le Harve 5/9/44 with bomb doors agape. Clearly showing are the dinghy stowage in the starboard wing, the walk lines and effects of exhausts. Note— very little stain from outboard exhausts due to dihedral. (Evidence in Camera)

Below: BIII ND527 LE–O 630 Squadron, East Kirkby, Summer 1944. Flown by Plt/Off. D. E. Hawker (RNZAF) and crew. Note coloured fin for daylight ops—colours uncertain. Several styles were tried out and one consisted of a broad black horizontal band on a dull maroon fin and rudder. (J. A. Warwick)

Left: BII DS622, SW–Q, 1678 Conversion Flight, Foulsham, 11/43. Note 'Mac' on the dorsal turret fairing, dating back to the aircraft's service with 115 Squadron.   (D. S. Beckwith)

Below: Lanc of the Special Duty Flight, Binbrook, mid 1944 Squadron unknown—but see text for examples. Note the crudely painted white identification bands which were also painted above and below the tailplanes.   (N. R. Truman)

*Post War markings—Bomber R.A.F.

*BVII (F.E.) NX678, WS-S 9 Squadron, Salbani, India, 10/2/46. In the cockpit is F/S. P. Grimwood rear gunner to Flt/Lt. P. G. Langdon. The unofficial squadron badge was not approved by 'Higher Authority' and was replaced by the standard R.A.F. pattern badge shown at right.   (P. Grimwood)

*Above: BVII (F.E.) NX784. WS-X 9 Squadron, Salbani, circa 3/46, sporting the official squadron badge. All badges were painted on by F/S. G. S. Shorthouse, Flight Engineer.   (W. Scott)

*Below: Indian Scene, BVII (F.E.) NX773, WS-M, 9 Squadron, Salbani, 2/46. Like many other squadrons, No. 9 revised the shape and style of it's codes post-war.   (W. E. Harrison)

*Above: BVII (F.E.) NX724, 'D' 37 Squadron, Shallufa, between 10/46 and 1/47. Flt/Lt. R. K. Moores and crew. Codes 'BL' still visible from previous service with 40 Squadron. At this stage No's. 37 and 38 Squadrons shared their Lancs. (R. K. Moores)

*Above: BVII (F.E.) NX727, RL-L, 38 Squadron, Ein Shemer 5/47. The code 'RL' was used by no fewer than 6 units as detailed under the A.S.R.III photographs. Codes in bright red. Note the wartime style exhaust shrouds and coloured engine top panels, possibly a protection against sand. (J. W. Patrick)

*Right: BI PP687, KM-W, 44 Squadron, Mildenhall, circa 10/45. Note how the engine exhaust has all but obliterated the '7' of the serial number. G-H bars still faintly visible from previous service with 149 Squadron. Hardly visible is the bulged bomb bay. Flt/Lt. P. J. Tupper and crew. (J. Chatterton)

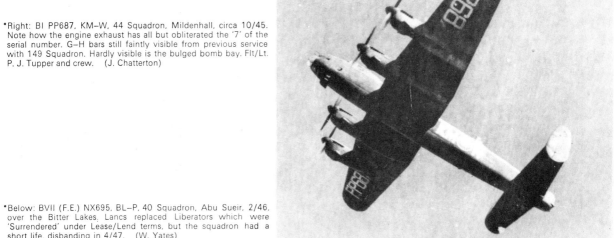

*Below: BVII (F.E.) NX695, BL-P, 40 Squadron, Abu Sueir, 2/46, over the Bitter Lakes. Lancs replaced Liberators which were 'Surrendered' under Lease/Lend terms, but the squadron had a short life, disbanding in 4/47. (W. Yates)

*Above & Left: Wintry Scene at Waddington. BIII ME359, 50 Squadron, 1/46. Flt/Lt. W. G. Rees in cockpit. Note unofficial squadron badge.
(W. G. Rees)

*Below: BI NG115, DX–C, 57 Squadron, Scampton, 1–2/46. Squadron badge just discernable. Note Rose-Rice rear turret—dating from previous service with 166 Sqaudron.   (R. E. Woods)

Below: BI PA329, QR–K, 61 Squadron, Sturgate, 6–8/45.   (E. Beswick)

1
BI L7571, OF–X. 97 (Straits Settlements) Squadron, Woodhall Spa, April 1942. It has the early type roundels & fin flash. The grey codes were phased out during May/June 1942.

2
BI R5677, ZN–A. "Admiral Chattanooga". 106 Squadron. Coningsby. Sept. 1942. Flown by Flt/Lt. W. N. Whamond (Rhodesia) & crew. Note non-standard roundels.

3
BII DS626, KO–J. 115 Squadron, East Wretham, March 1943. Flown by Sgt. G. P. Finnerty (R.C.A.F.) & crew. Motif painted by F/S. W. B. Baker the mid-upper gunner.

4
BIII (Special) ED912, AJ–S. 617 Squadron. Coningsby. December 1943. Flown by Flt/Lt. R. S. D. Kearns (R.N.Z.A.F.) & crew. Originally flown by Flt/Lt. L. G. Knight (R.A.A.F.) on the Dams Raid, as AJ–N. The identity letter changed from 'N' to 'S' on 22/11/43. The "Saint" motif was painted on all Kearns' kites.

5
BIII ED623, UM–M². 626 Squadron, Wickenby, April 1944. Flown by Fg/Off. D. J. Henty & crew. It still has the early shallow bomb aimer's blister & port cockpit observation blister.

Roffe

1
BIII LM378, PG–J. 619 Squadron. Dunholme Lodge, April 1944. Flown by Fg/Off. K. M. Roberts (R.A.A.F.) & crew.

2
BI LL757, SR–W. "Oor Wullie". 101 Squadron, Ludford Magna, May/June 1944. Flown by Plt/Off. R. R. Waughman & crew. Equipped with A.B.C. "Airborne Cigar" jamming equipment. Note Rose-Rice tail turret. 'SR' forward of roundel, on starboard side.

3
BI NG142, A2–H. "The Lancashire Lass". 514 Squadron, Waterbeach, Oct./Nov. 1944. Flown by Fg/Off. F. Heald & crew Whereas 'A' & 'B' Flights used the code 'J1', 'C' Flight used A2.

4
BIII PB513, LQ–H. 405 ("Vancouver") Squadron. R.C.A.F., Gransden Lodge, Nov. 1944. Flown by Sqn/Ldr. L. B. Burnand (R.C.A.F.) & crew. Note rear vision blister under nose.

5
BX KB831, SE–E. 431 ("Iroquois") Squadron, R.C.A.F., Croft, Nov. 1944. Flown by Fg/Off. B. M. Kaplansky (R.C.A.F.) & crew.

Roffe

1
BI RF144, EM–H. 207 Squadron. Spilsby March, 1945. Flown by Fg/Off. R. S. Halewood (R.A.A.F.) & crew. Note the yellow-outlined codes, introduced by 5 Group post D–Day.

2
BIII ME545, XH–L. "Lovely Lou" 218 (Gold Coast) Squadron, Chedburgh, April/May 1945. Flown by Flt/Lt. H. F. Warwick & crew. 'A' & 'B' Flights used the code 'HA' & 'C' Flight 'XH'. G–H Leader. Note absence of 3 Group gas patch.

3
BI PA221, HW–V & V². "Vergeltungswaffe" (Revenge Weapon). 100 Squadron, Elsham Wolds April 1945. Flown by Flt/Lt. W. F. Spowage & crew. When the squadron was at Waltham (it moved to Elsham Wolds 1/4/45) this machine was HW–V. Note 1 Group's Gas–Disc.

4
BI PA308, AS–W. 166 Squadron, Kirmington, Aug. 1945, showing a mixture of wartime & post war markings, typical of the period of re-adjustment. Note Rose-Rice tail turret & bulged bomb bay.

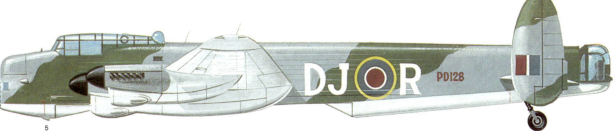

5
BI (Special) PD128, DJ–R. 15 Squadron, Mildenhall, Sept. 1945, in a mixture of wartime & post war markings. 'C' Flight used code 'DJ' while 'A' & 'B' used 'LS'. Aircraft & crews were transferred from 617 Squadron to undertake bombing trials alongside the B–29 Superfortress.

1

BIII JA845, FCX–T. Empire Flying School, Hullavington, Autumn 1946. Built in July 1943 this Lanc. still has the early position pitot head & an impressive number of bomb symbols faintly visible on the nose. 'FCX' appeared aft of roundels on stbd. side. Badge both sides of nose.

2

BI (F/E) TW657, TL–C. 35 (Madras Presidency) Squadron, Graveley, as on the Squadron's tour of the U.S.A. in July 1946. The black/white finish was originally introduced for service in the Pacific. The badge appeared on both sides of the nose, the horse facing forward in each case.

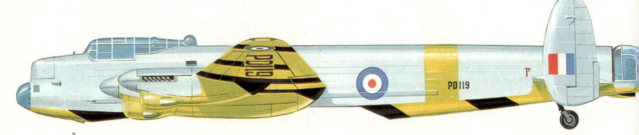

3

BI (Special) PD119. Used as a target tug, etc., at the Royal Aircraft Establishment, Farnborough 1948/9 & probably the only Lanc. so adorned.

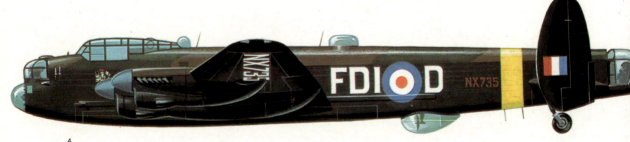

4

BVII NX735, FD1–D. Central Flying School, Little Rissington 1949. While some machines of this unit wore camouflage, others were in natural metal or the black/white (F/E) scheme. Badge both sides of nose.

5

PRI RA626, ('S'). 683 Squadron, a unit which operated all over the Near and Middle East on photographic survey work 1951 to 1954. The Squadron badge appeared on both sides of the nose. 'S' carried forward of roundel on stbd. side.

Roffe

1
ASRIII RF313, RL–F. 1348 Flight, Pegu, Burma, Feb. 1946. The camouflage was phased out in 1949/50 & replaced by the grey/white scheme shown below on RE207.

2
GR3 RE207, BS–D. 120 Squadron, Kinloss, late 1948. Various coloured spinners were applied to the Squadron's Lancs. at different times. No badge on nose at this time.

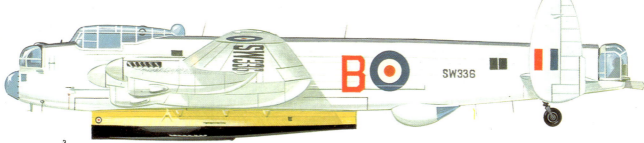

3
GR3 SW336, ('B'). 37 Squadron, Luqa, Malta 1950, carrying one of several types of lifeboat used. No badge on nose though most of the Squadron's Lancs. had same. 'B' aft of roundels on stbd. side.

4
MR3 SW374 ('Z'). 38 Squadron, Luqa, Malta, 1952/53. Squadron badge on both sides of nose. 'Z' aft of roundels on stbd. side. By this time the code letters had been dropped. The underwing roundel was also being dropped about this time.

5
MR3 SW367, H–X. School of Maritime Reconnaissance, St. Mawgan 1956, in the scheme introduced on the Shackleton. 'H' aft on stbd. side. From 1951 unit codes became single letters. The unit's badge appeared on both sides of the nose.

Rolfe

1
B7 NX739. Operated by Eagle Aviation at Blackbushe on Ministry of Supply photographic work. Shown in its final guise 1956/7 and probably the only Lanc. ever to have the black/grey scheme as on the Lincoln. The Eagle was carried on both sides of the nose. Note bulged bomb bay—a left over from service with 617 Squadron.

2
10–MR FM220, AF–K. 404 ("Buffalo") Squadron, R.C.A.F., Greenwood, Nova Scotia 1952. The badge appeared on the port side only.

3
10–P FM199, MN–199. 408 ("Goose") Squadron, R.C.A.F., Rockcliffe, Ottawa, mid 1950s. Note the use of the 'Last Three' of the serial number for identification in the air. Sqdn. badge on port side only.

4
10–AR KB976, MN–976. 408 ("Goose") Squadron, R.C.A.F., Rockcliffe, 1959/60. The ultimate Canadian version, for Arctic photographic survey work (note lengthened nose). This machine made the last flight by an operational Lanc. (April 1964). No unit badge at this time.

5
10–MR FM213 ('213'). 107 Rescue Unit, Torbay, Newfoundland, 1963. Showing the ultimate scheme applied to Canadian Lancs. This machine was selected for preservation.

Roffe

1
MR7 WU14. 55s–F of Escadrille de Servitude 55s L'Aeronavale, Agadir, Morocco, mid 1950s. Formerly BVII NX623.
No unit badge carried.

2
MR1 WU27. of '9s' Noumea, New Caledonia, 1963. The unit badge appeared on both sides of the nose. Formerly B1
TW651, it is unique in being one of the few Mk. Is converted to MR standard.

3
MR7 105–Q. Operated on air-sea rescue duties in North Africa in the 1950s. Flown by the French equivalent of the
Coast Guard. Formerly FCL–05 & BVII RT679.

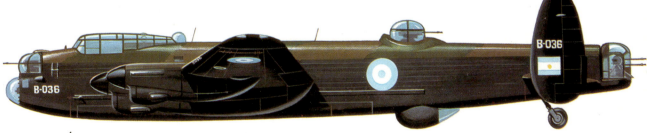

4
B1 B–036. Argentinian Air Force. Delivered Dec. 1948, it originally carried the temporary civil registration G–11–19.
Formerly PA349.

5
B1 1808. Royal Egyptian Air Force, delivered October 1950. Formerly SW313 and originally allotted the temporary civil
registration G–11–61.

Roffe

Nose emblems and badges appearing on aircraft illustrated on colour pages

see side view **B4**

see side view **A3**

see side view **A4**

Ali Oop
see side view **A5**

see side view **B1**

OOR WULLIE
see side view **B2**

see side view **F1**

ADMIRAL CHATTANOOGA
see side view **A2**

see side view **D2**

see side view **B5**

see side view **G2**

see side view **E5**

see side view **B3**

see side view **C2**

see side view **C3**

see side view **D5**

see side view **F2**

see side view **F3**

see side view **E4**

see side view **D1 and D4**

Above: BVII (F.E.) NX737, 'C' 70 Squadron, El Kabrit, 8–9/46, or Shallufa, 9/46–1/47. Another Liberator Squadron, 70 reformed at Fayid in April 1946 from 178 Squadron but only survived for a year. (R. G. Ashford)

Above: PRI TW884, 'B' Roberts Field, Liberia, 1946. 82 Squadron reformed from 541 Squadron at Accra 9–10/46 and this Lanc was used by both squadrons. Red codes and serials on fuselage. (A. Lloyd)

Below: PRI PA439, 'D' 82 Squadron, Eastleigh, circa 1949/50 in natural metal finish adopted in place of the F.E. scheme shown on TW884. (R. A. Cooper)

Below: BIII ND824, OL-G, 83 Squadron, Coningsby, seen at Pomigliano 11/45, on operation "Dodge"—bringing back soldiers from Italy. (F. E. Harper)

Above: BVII (F.E.) NX736, EP–E, 104 Squadron, Abu Sueir, 1946, over the Suez Canal. Another former Liberator Squadron, 104 did not last long and disbanded at the end of March 1947.   (D. S. Richardson)

Below: BI PA181, KO–A, 115 Squadron, Witchford, circa 6/45. Though the post war white serial has been painted under the wings the codes have not yet been re-painted white and remain dull red.   (D. West)

Below: BI (F.E.) TW908, 'AU–U', 148 Squadron, Upwood, seen at Shallufa in 1948, on a "Sunray" exercise. Note difference in paint partition line on starboard engines.   (Syndication International) (Odhams)

Right: BIII SW359, J–178 Squadron, Fayid, 1946. Having been a mixed Halifax/Liberator squadron. 178 only had Lancs from Nov. 1945 until April 1946 when it was re-numbered 70 Squadron. No codes were used but aircraft carried a 'Bar' over identity letters. (R. G. Ashford)

Above: BI (F.E's) TW893, 'R' (Flt/Lt. F. J. Wheeler) and TW891, NF–K (Flt/Lt R. M. Horsley), 138 Squadron, Wyton, 18/4/47 on operation "Rufus", one of many post-war exercises. TW893 has yet to have the 'NF' codes painted on, after transfer from 115 Squadron.   (Flight International)

Left: Close up of FN82 rear turret.   (A. D. Clayton)

Below: BI (F.E.) TW869, EM–D, 207 Squadron, Stradishall, returning from a "Sunray" exercise at Shallufa, July 1947. Note how the serial prefix letters are carried above the number—a feature of a few BI (F.E's)   (R. Wood)

Above: BI (F.E.) TW882, QN–V, 214 (Federated Malay States) Squadron, Upwood, 14/12/48. The shadow of the tail gives the impression of a fuselage band. Note serial behind door.   (A. D Clayton)

Right: BVII (F.E.) NX739, KC–Q, 617 Squadron, Waddington, shortly before the squadron went to India in January 1946. See colour illustration of this Lanc in later guise. Note early appearance of Lincoln rudders. (N. H. Frost)

Below: PRI TW652 'P', 683 Squadron, over Jerusalem, 8/52. 683 ranged far and wide over the Middle East on photographic survey work.   (A. E. Smale)

†ASRIII SW288, RL-G, at Istres-le-Tube, France, 15–17 January 1946. The Lanc Flight of 279 Squadron, Thornaby-on-Tees, was renamed 1348 flight, despatched to Pegu, Burma, arriving 28/1/46, but disbanded 17/4/46. Aircraft and crews transferred to Aqir, Palestine, to become the Lanc flight of 621 Squadron. 621 in turn was renumbered 18 Squadron 1/9/46 at Ein Shemer, but the latter lasted only until 14/9/46 & was absorbed into 38 Squadron. The code 'RL' was handed down from unit to unit. (J. W. Patrick)

†Below: ASRIII RF322, RL-J, 621 Squadron, Aqir, Circa 6/46. At this stage the lifeboats carried were of the MkII type, as fitted to the Warwick. (J. W. Patrick)

†Below: ASRIII SW293, RL-B, 37 Squadron, Luqa, Malta, Circa 1949. 37's badge consisting of a hooded, belled & fessed hunting hawk is here seen in unofficial form. (P. Clifton)

†Below: MR3 RF273, 'T' 38 Squadron, Luqa, seen at Fayid in 1953. This was destined to be the last Lanc in front line service with the RAF. Underwing roundels dispensed with by this time, as was 38's squadron badge. Note Lincoln under-carriage, wheels & rudders. (R. Dodd)

†Coastal

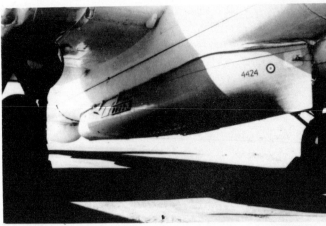

†Above & Left: Close ups of MR3, RF273, 'T' 38 Squadron. Note the small roundel on the lifeboat, which appeared on both sides of the bow. (R. Dodd)

†Below: GRIII BS–H, (Probably PB529), 120 Squadron, Leuchars, 1949. Though most aircraft carried the codes 'BS' forward of the Roundel on the port side, odd examples did not—as shown. 120's badge (an owl) was 'mounted' in a disc, though not all their Lancs carried it. (G. A. Perfect)

†Below: GRIII SW364, CJ–C, 203 Squadron, St. Eval, circa 1949/50. The 'Shute' protruding from the tail housed a rear facing camera, while the object on the bomb bay is the lifeboat attachment. (203 Squadron)

†Left: GRIII RF307, OZ–W, 210 Squadron, St. Eval, circa 1948. 'OZ' was originally used by 179 Squadron which had exchanged Warwicks for Lancs in Feb. 1946. Under an experimental scheme 179 was split into 179X & 179Y Squadrons but this proved unsatisfactory and in June 1946 the latter became 210 Squadron.   (G. Raggett)

†Below: MR3, L–W, 210 Squadron, photographed at Aldergrove, 1952, shortly before the unit received Neptunes. The Green/Grey camouflage scheme was phased out in 1949/50 and replaced by the Grey/White scheme shown here. The two–letter codes were changed to single letter in late 1950.
(Avro)

†Above: GRIII RF325, P9–J, of the ASWDU, Thorney Island. Destined to be the last Lanc in RAF service, and is pictured again later in service with the SMR   (E. W. Watts)

†Left: Nose of a 'pranged' 210 Squadron Lanc showing the squadron badge, albeit in unofficial form.   (G. Raggett)

†Below: ASRIII PB529, XB–F, 224 Squadron, St. Eval, 9/47. Whereas most ASRIII's were new Lancs from storage this example had seen much service with three units as a BIII.
(J. D. R. Rawlings)

†Above: GRIII RE200, K7–K, 236 OCU, Kinloss, 12/49. Note the serial above the tailplane and no white leading edge on wings. (A. J. L. Craig)

†Above: GRIII RF318, K7–LB, 236 OCU, Kinloss, between 10/48 & 1/49. Note different code placing and that only the 'B' of 'LB' is carried on the nose. This aircraft, too, has grey leading edges. The 'L' stood for 'Lancaster'. (A. B. Walker)

†Left: MR3 RF303, H–F, School of Maritime Reconnaissance, St. Mawgan, 1952. Compare depth of grey down fuselage side with that of RF325 shown below. White leading edges. No unit badge at this stage. (A. B. Walker)

†Below: MR3 RE186, H–L, SMR, in the 'Blue-Grey' overall scheme introduced on the Shackleton, but with interim white codes and serials. For ultimate scheme see colour illustration E5. (M. J. Hibbert)

†Below: MR3 RF325, H–D, SMR., St. Mawgan, 11/11/53 during exercise "Mariner". For this exercise orange and yellow bands (in distemper) were painted on fuselage and wing tips. This Lanc became the last in RAF service. Early SMR badge on nose. (A. B. Walker)

● Above: BI LM224, FGF-B, ("Libra") Empire Air Navigation School, Shawbury, here seen at Changi, Singapore, late 1945. The EANS Lancs were the first to shed their camouflage, first done on the famous PD 328 "Aries". Whereas "Aries" was a special 'one-off' machine, "Libra" was not. (D. H. Taylor)

● **Miscellaneous—RAF Post-war**

● Left: BI LL795, TV-Q, 1660 HCU, Swinderby. Here seen at Cambridge in 1947. (C. E. Shadbolt)

● Left: BIII ME315, 2K-L, seen at North Luffenham, on transfer from 1668 CU Cottesmore (whose codes it bears in wartime red) to 1653 CU, whose Lancs are seen in the background (coded 'A3' in post-war white). While on 'ops' with 405 Squadron. ME315 had its rear turret shot off by an ME262. The band round the fuselage is the patched joint of the D3/D4 sections, the aircraft probably receiving a complete new rear (D4) section after the incident. (J. Couch)

● Right: BI (F.E.) PA380, V7-B, of the Central Signals Establishment, Watton, seen in Malta, circa 1949. (P. Clifton)

● Right: BVII (F.E.) RT680, FCX-S, Empire Flying School, Hullavington, 24/4/48. Note yellow training band and also the still faintly visible former yellow outer ring to the roundel. Serial is immediately in front of tailplane. (L. S. Vowles)

● Above: BVII (F.E.) NX721, FGG–A, Empire Air Navigation School, Shawbury, visiting Waddington, 12/8/48. Martin dorsal turret replaced by astrodome.   (R. Sturtivant)

★Above: 10–MR KB890, SP–890, 404 ("Buffalo") Squadron, RCAF, from Greenwood, Nova Scotia. 404 used both 'AF' and 'SP' codes.   (C. Holland)

★Post war RCAF and other users

★Above: 10–MR KB950, AG–L, 405 ("Vancouver)" Squadron, RCAF, from Greenwood, Nova Scotia, photographed at Northolt, UK, 6/6/51. Codes repeated on top of, and below, the wings.
(L. S. Vowles)

★Right: Nose close up of KB950
(L. S. Vowles)

★Above: 10–MR KB919, DJ–D, Eastern Air Command, Greenwood, Nova Scotia, at Northolt 21/6/51. Possibly 405 Squadron.
(L. S. Vowles)

★Above: 10–MP FM159, RX–159, 407 ("Demon") Squadron, RCAF, from Comox, British Colombia, at Prestwick, UK. Now preserved in Canada. Under surface was "High Speed" grey.   (Haydn Hurst)

★Above & below: 10–AR KB882. One of three Lancs specially modified for aerial and Arctic reconnaissance (note lengthened nose) and used by 408 ("Goose") Squadron, RCAF, at Rockcliffe, Ottawa, 1963/4. By this time the codes 'MN' had been dropped and the overall markings revised.   (Canadian Forces Photos)

✸ Above: 10–MP FM104, CX–104, 107 Rescue Unit, Torbay, Newfoundland, in an early paint scheme. Here seen at Prestwick, U.K. (M. Gibbon)

✸ Left & below: Close up views of 10–MP FM104, 107 Rescue Unit, Torbay, in a later scheme. This Lanc is preserved in Canada. (G. Anderson)

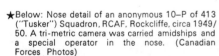

★ Below: Nose detail of an anonymous 10–P of 413 ("Tusker") Squadron, RCAF, Rockcliffe, circa 1949/50. A tri-metric camera was carried amidships and a special operator in the nose. (Canadian Forces Photos)

★Above: WU33 (exBl PA477) of Escadrille de Servitude 56S L'Aeronavale, Agadir, Morocco, at Dakar 11/59. (R. Caratini/J. M. G. Gradidge)

★Right & below: WU01 (ex BVII NX613) of 10S, St. Raphael, (S. France) a test unit, Photograph on right at Luqa, mid 1950's with U.S. APS radar, prior to Neptune conversion; and below, the same aircraft at Dakar, 11/59. Note mixed GR/MR standard —Lincoln undercarriage, Lanc rudders. (R. C. B. Ashworth,/ R. Caratini,/J. M. G. Gradidge)

★Left: WU41 (ex Bl TW928) of 9S Noumea, New Caledonia, in the 1950's, in tropical white finish. This unit did not give up it's Lancs until 1964. (E.C.A.)

★Above: 103–N (ex BVII RT689) one of five Mk. 7's sold to France for rescue duties in the Mediterranean and Eastern Atlantic by the French equivalent of the British Coast Guard—seen at Dakar 11/59. Originally coded FCL03 (R. Caratini/J. M. G. Gradidge)

★Above: BI PA377 as B–O33 for the Argentine Air Force, photographed at Langar 12/6/48 prior to delivery. (R. Sturtivant)

★Below: BI SW313 as 1808 for the Royal Egyptian Air Force, staging through Luqa, Malta, Oct 1950 on delivery. The "Avro" badge can be seen below the fin flash.   (A. B. Walker)

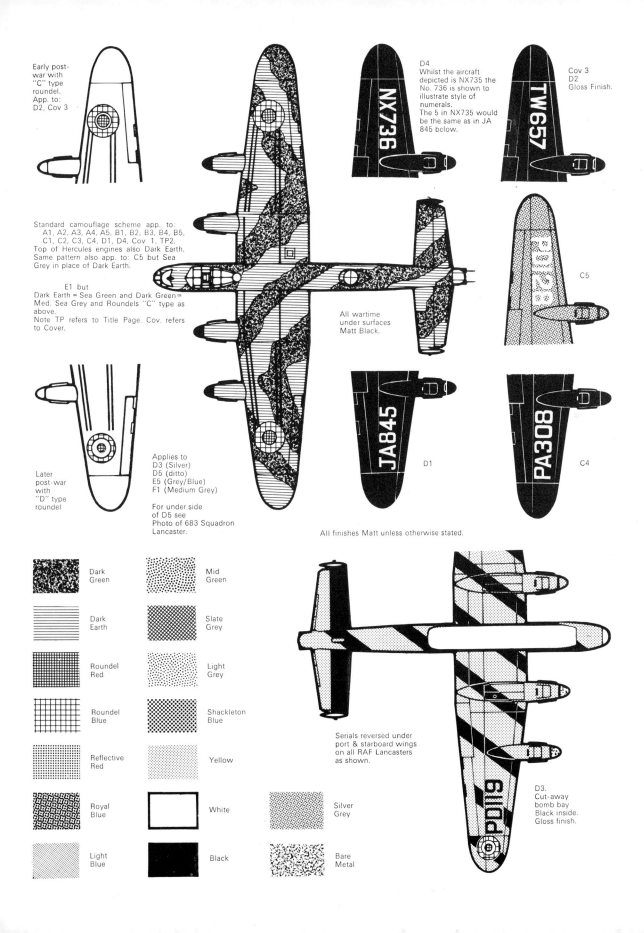

Early post-war with "C" type roundel. App. to: D2, Cov 3

Standard camouflage scheme app. to: A1, A2, A3, A4, A5, B1, B2, B3, B4, B5, C1, C2, C3, C4, D1, D4, Cov 1, TP2. Top of Hercules engines also Dark Earth. Same pattern also app. to: C5 but Sea Grey in place of Dark Earth.

E1 but
Dark Earth = Sea Green and Dark Green = Med. Sea Grey and Roundels "C" type as above.
Note TP refers to Title Page. Cov. refers to Cover.

Later post-war with "D" type roundel

Applies to)
D3 (Silver)
D5 (ditto)
E5 (Grey/Blue)
F1 (Medium Grey)

For under side of D5 see Photo of 683 Squadron Lancaster.

D4
Whilst the aircraft depicted is NX735 the No. 736 is shown to illustrate style of numerals. The 5 in NX735 would be the same as in JA 845 below.

Cov 3
D2
Gloss Finish.

NX736

TW657

All wartime under surfaces Matt Black.

C5

JA845   D1

PA308   C4

All finishes Matt unless otherwise stated.

Dark Green	Mid Green
Dark Earth	Slate Grey
Roundel Red	Light Grey
Roundel Blue	Shackleton Blue
Reflective Red	Yellow
Royal Blue	White
Light Blue	Black
	Silver Grey
	Bare Metal

Serials reversed under port & starboard wings on all RAF Lancasters as shown.

PD119

D3.
Cut-away bomb bay Black inside. Gloss finish.

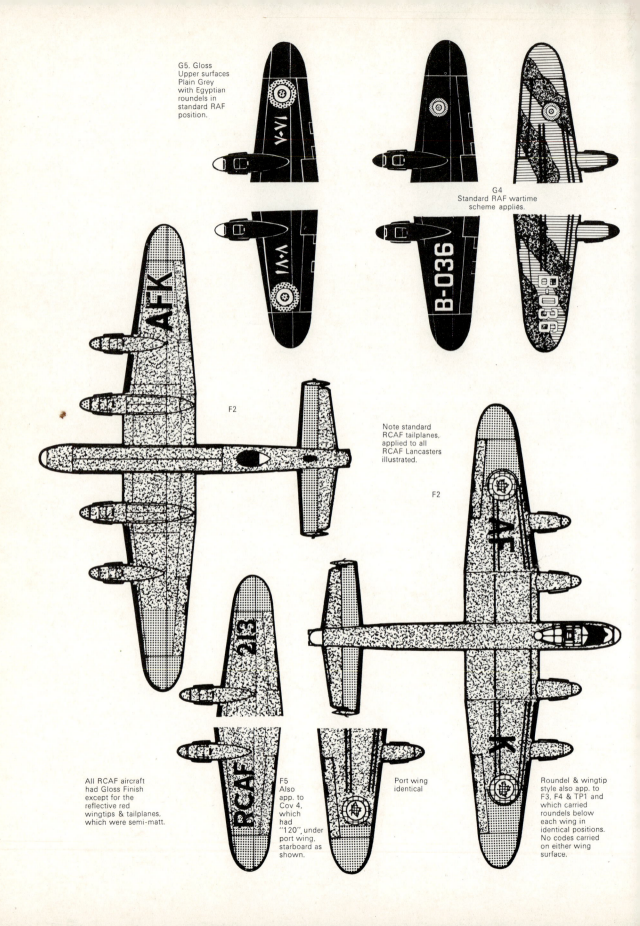

G5. Gloss
Upper surfaces
Plain Grey
with Egyptian
roundels in
standard RAF
position.

G4
Standard RAF wartime
scheme applies.

F2

Note standard
RCAF tailplanes,
applied to all
RCAF Lancasters
illustrated.

F2

All RCAF aircraft
had Gloss Finish
except for the
reflective red
wingtips & tailplanes,
which were semi-matt.

F5
Also
app. to
Cov 4,
which
had
"120", under
port wing,
starboard as
shown.

Port wing
identical

Roundel & wingtip
style also app. to
F3, F4 & TP1 and
which carried
roundels below
each wing in
identical positions.
No codes carried
on either wing
surface.